a gift for:

_____

from:

_____

Published by Hallmark Books,
a division of Hallmark Cards, Inc.,
Kansas City, MO 64141
Visit us on the Web at www.Hallmark.com.

Editor: Theresa Trinder
Art Director: Kevin Swanson
Designer & Production Artist: Dan C. Horton

ISBN: 978-1-59530-268-7

BOK4361

Printed and bound in China

How Sweet It Is

Being Grandma

by **Myra Zirkle** • illustrated by **Elissa Hudson**

Hallmark
GIFT BOOKS

You're a wise woman
with a wealth of knowledge
and a world of experience.

And just when you thought you'd seen it all . . .
you became a grandmother.

And since then,
nothing has been the same.

Isn't it amazing

how such a little person

can make such a big difference?

Grandma, Nana, Bubbie, Grams . . .

whatever your grandchild
decides to call you,
it's the sweetest word in the world.

You were never one to brag . . .
but showing off is part of
a grandma's job description.

Before your grandchild
came along, you may not
have fully understood
why the picture frame was invented.

Saturday morning cartoons
give you the giggles.

Children's books are fun to read again.
And again
    and again
        and again!

And you're pretty sure
the phone was invented
just so a little voice
could call to say
"I love you."

When it comes to art,

you know what you like.

And there's always room for more.

You get asked the most
wonderful questions, like . . .

"Was there a sky when you were a little girl?"

There's always someone there
to remind you
that sometimes it's okay
to stop and pick the dandelions.

Cartwheels and training wheels
and "Watch this!" times one hundred
gives you lots of practice at
oohing and ahhing.

You amuse yourself
and amaze your friends . . .

with everything you know
about superheroes.

You never thought you'd have to
do show-and-tell ever again . . .

but that's what family photo albums are for!

Their favorites, of course,
are the stories where Mommy (or Daddy) . . .

was NOT a very good girl (or boy).

Doing homework,

doing chores,

doing nothing much at all . . .

if you're doing it together,

it's extraordinary.

Thanks to a grandkid, you can . . .

upload photos

video chat

text

e-mail

LOL

or some really impressive

combination of the above.

There's always someone
who really, really wants to
sit next to you at the table.

You've never felt so important . . .
from the first enormous hug
to the last wistful
"Do you have to go?"

Sure, you have favorites.

However many grandchildren there are . . .

that's how many favorites you have.

You find yourself saying things
you never did before,
like, "How BIG you're getting!
I hope this hug still fits!"

All those rules you made
when you raised your own kids
won't seem so important
this time around.

You become really, really good
at pretending you never, ever heard
that knock-knock joke before.

Grandkids keep you sharp!
It's all that thinking up new ways
to let them be the winner.

"*You* can't always get
what you want . . ."

is not always true

for your grandkids.

"Just because"
is the only occasion you need
to give a grandkid a present.

Is there anything sweeter
than a teeny tiny pair of shoes?

You also learn
it isn't always fun and games.

Nothing makes your heart hurt more
than when your grandchild
is feeling sad.

But you can tell them,
because you know that it is true,
that hurt does not stay forever . . .

and happy feels happier
than ever before.

You keep pen and paper handy
because you never know
when that cute little voice
will say something
uncommonly wise.

*Y*ou believe in them
and tell them so,

and your grandchildren get taller
right before your eyes.

In their lifetime, they'll learn
there are a million different kinds of love.

And you'll help them learn
that the best kind
is the forever kind . . .

with no conditions
and no strings.

And, as if that weren't enough,
you get another chance
to notice all the magic in the world.

Whether it's right at your feet . . .

or all around you . . .

or up where dreams are just taking shape.

When you're holding
your grandchild's hand,
tomorrow looks like
a beautiful place to be headed for.

$\mathcal{I}$f you have enjoyed this book
or it has touched your life in some way,
we would love to hear from you.

Please send your comments to:

Hallmark Book Feedback
P.O. Box 419034
Mail Drop 215
Kansas City, MO 64141

or e-mail us:

booknotes@hallmark.com